AF228193

EXPLORING NATURE

Spotting Flowers

BY LAURA PERDEW

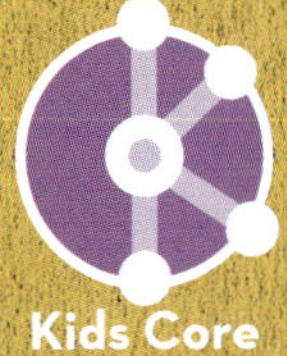

Kids Core
An Imprint of Abdo Publishing
abdobooks.com

abdobooks.com

Published by Abdo Publishing, a division of ABDO, PO Box 398166, Minneapolis, Minnesota 55439. Copyright © 2026 by Abdo Consulting Group, Inc. International copyrights reserved in all countries. No part of this book may be reproduced in any form without written permission from the publisher. Kids Core™ is a trademark and logo of Abdo Publishing.

Printed in the United States of America, North Mankato, Minnesota.
102025
012026

Cover Photo: Cat Simpson/Shutterstock Images
Interior Photos: Danita Delimont/Shutterstock Images, 4–5; Russell Illig/Photographer's Choice RF/Getty Images, 7; Marcin Rogozinski/Shutterstock Images, 8; Mango Productions/Stone/Getty Images, 10–11; Brian Woolman/Shutterstock Images, 12; Ludmila Kapustkina/Shutterstock Images, 13; Laura Perdew, 14; Danica Chang/Shutterstock Images, 16; Shutterstock Images, 17, 20–21, 28 (top right), 28 (bottom left), 29; Irina Sergeyeva/Shutterstock Images, 18; Mike Truchon/Shutterstock Images, 23; Havryliuk Kharzhevska/Shutterstock Images, 24; Maria Symchych/Shutterstock Images, 26; Irina Gutyryak/Shutterstock Images, 28 (top left); Tetiana Rostopira/Shutterstock Images, 28 (bottom right)

Editor: Marie Pearson
Series Designer: Marley Richmond

Library of Congress Control Number: 2025939129

Publisher's Cataloging-in-Publication Data

Names: Perdew, Laura, author.
Title: Spotting flowers / by Laura Perdew
Description: Minneapolis, Minnesota: Abdo Publishing, 2026 | Series: Exploring nature | Includes online resources and index.
Identifiers: ISBN 9781098298715 (lib. bdg.) | ISBN 9798384932512 (ebook)
Subjects: LCSH: Flowering plants--Juvenile literature. | Wild flowers--Juvenile literature. | Botany--Juvenile literature. | Nature--Juvenile literature. | Ecological science--Juvenile literature. | Habitats (Ecology)--Juvenile literature.
Classification: DDC 580.7--dc23

CONTENTS

The black-eyed Susan grows
in almost all of the US states.

CHAPTER 1

A Field of Flowers

Zeny and her family rounded a bend in the trail. She could not believe her eyes. The open field was filled with yellow wildflowers! Some were chest high on her.

Zeny knelt on the trail. She was eye to eye with a flower.

It was yellow with a brown center. She counted the petals, which were arranged like spokes on a bicycle wheel. The stem was a bit hairy. The leaves were like long ovals with a bit of a point on one end. The leaves also had jagged edges. Zeny sketched the flower in her notebook.

At home, Zeny pulled out the drawing. She opened a field guide and found the flower.

Protecting Wildflowers

Wildflowers can grow without human help. But they are also fragile. Camping on, stepping on, or having a picnic on top of wildflowers can kill them. If flowers are picked, the plant cannot reproduce. If wildflowers are harmed, animals lose food and shelter, and the soil may wash away more easily.

She wrote its name, black-eyed Susan, on her picture.

What Are Flowers?

Flowers are parts of a plant that help the plant reproduce. Some, such as the black-eyed Susan, grow without any help from people. These are called wildflowers.

Bumblebees are among the many pollinator species that rely on flowers.

Wildflowers grow in many types of **habitats** all over the world. Some wildflowers, such as forget-me-nots, can be tiny. These flowers can be as small as 0.25 inches (0.64 cm) wide. Wildflowers can also be huge like sunflowers, with heads larger than a dinner plate.

Wildflowers come in many shapes. Some have petals that spread out from the center like the black-eyed Susan. Others are tube shaped, such as foxglove. Flowers also come in a variety of colors.

Wildflowers are important to their habitats. They support **pollinators**. They provide food and shelter for small animals. Wildflowers help keep soil healthy. Their roots prevent soil from washing away. Many people enjoy looking for wildflowers while exploring the outdoors!

Further Evidence

Look at the website below. Does it give any new evidence to support Chapter One?

Why We Need Wildflowers

abdocorelibrary.com/spotting-flowers

Some people go hiking to find wildflowers.

CHAPTER 2

Looking for Flowers

Wildflowers are found in most habitats around the world. There are wildflowers in wetlands, grasslands, and high mountain areas. Wildflowers grow along shorelines. Pink lady's slippers and fairy bells grow in forests.

Flowers such as desert lilies and scarlet gilia grow in the desert.

Wildflowers can be spotted growing in neighborhood parks and other natural spaces too. Daisies, pepperweed, and sunflowers are common. Many people also plant native wildflowers in their gardens. Plants such as milkweed and coneflowers help support pollinators.

Monarch butterflies eat the nectar of milkweed flowers. Monarch caterpillars eat milkweed leaves.

Some wildflowers, such as daisies, are used in landscaping at parks and around buildings.

Timing

The type of wildflowers blooming depends on the season, climate, and location. Flowers do not grow in the winter in colder climates.

However, warmer climates have different flowers that bloom throughout the year. In Florida, winter jasmine and some snapdragons bloom in the winter.

In other locations, flowers begin to bloom in March. Crocuses and spring beauties are often some of the first to bloom. People can spot other types of flowers too. Spring is the best time to see prickly pear cactus flowers in the desert. Wildflower season ends in the fall in most places. People might spot asters, bearded beggarticks, or old man's whiskers at this time of year.

Superbloom

A superbloom is a rare natural event. It occurs when an unusual number of wildflowers bloom at the same time. Superblooms happen in dry climates after a season with a lot of rain. Then, vast areas become carpeted with colorful flowers.

Elevation also affects when flowers bloom. Higher elevations are colder and can be covered in snow late into the spring. Sometimes flowers can be spotted only in July and August.

Tools for Spotting Flowers

Parks often have maps and information about where flowers are located. Some people use

Wildflowers begin blooming in the Colorado mountains in late May or early June.

A magnifying glass can help with counting petals or seeing the texture of a leaf.

mobile apps to locate and identify flowers. People might carry a magnifying glass to look closely at wildflowers. A ruler or tape measure can be used to measure flowers, leaves, and plant height.

A flower field guide contains pictures of many flowers. People can identify flowers they find by comparing them with the images in the book.

Some people carry a flower identification book. A camera can help people keep track of the flowers they see. So can a sketchbook.

Kim, who works at the North Carolina Arboretum, likes flowers. She said:

> The flower is one of the greatest inventions nature has ever made. They can be bright, showy, and flashy or tiny, hidden, and **camouflaged**. They can have amazing floral scents like honeysuckle, or they can smell rotten like trilliums.

Source: "Nature Nook: Wildflowers." *YouTube*, uploaded by Eco Explore, 22 Mar. 2021, youtube.com. Accessed 21 Apr. 2025.

Point of View

What is Kim's point of view on flowers? What is your point of view? Write a short essay about how your views are similar and different.

Learning about flowers helps
people enjoy the nature
around them.

Identifying Flowers

Identifying wildflowers takes practice. One of the first things to note is the habitat where the flower is growing. The time of year and location also help with flower identification. The height of the plant provides another clue.

Another way to identify a flower is by its shape. If its petals spread out from the center, people can count how many petals it has. How the petals are shaped and how they are arranged around the center give more clues. Other flowers can be shaped like a tube, trumpet, or bell. The flower's color and size can also help with identification.

Next, people look at how the flowers are arranged on the stem. Some flowering plants have a single flower per stem. Others have two flowers or clusters. In addition, the stem itself gives information. Some stems are smooth and waxy. Others are hairy.

Some flowers, such as Dutchman's breeches, have especially unique shapes.

Parts of a Flower

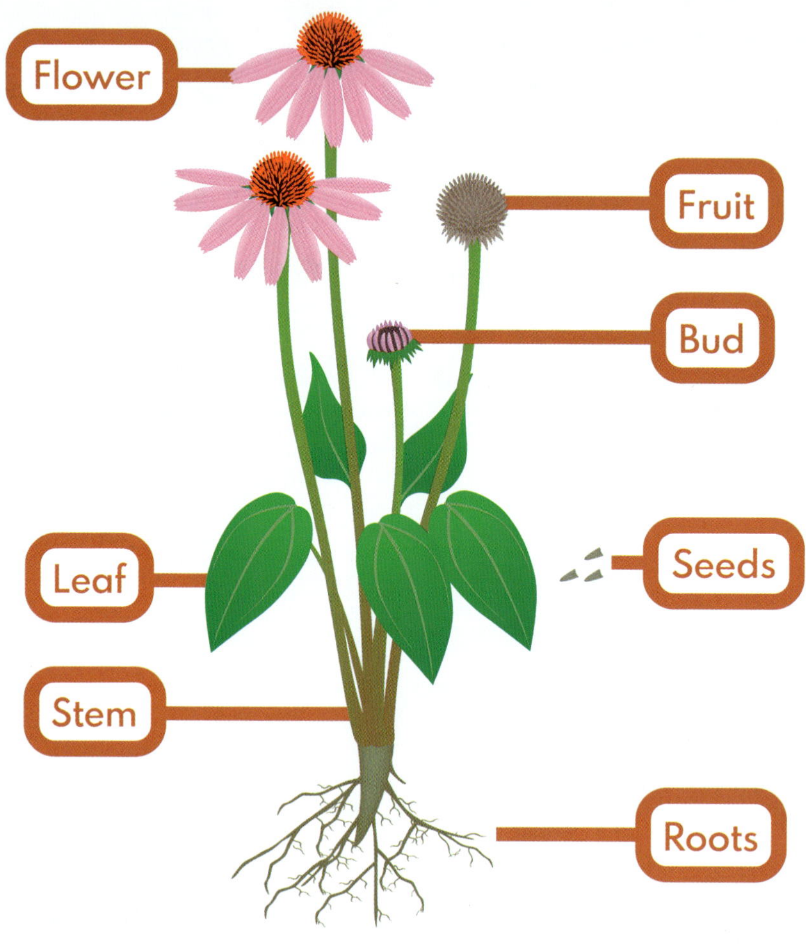

People can identify flowers by looking at their individual parts.

Leaves are important to look at too. People note leaf size and shape. Some leaves have smooth edges. Others have jagged edges.

Some leaves are long and thin, while others are round.

People check how the leaves are arranged on the stem. There might be one leaf or many extending from a certain point. Leaves could be arranged opposite each other or staggered on the stem. Finally, people note the **texture** of the leaves. They might be hairy, smooth, waxy, or prickly.

Alpine Wildflowers

Alpine wildflowers have **adaptations** that help them survive harsh conditions. Most grow low to the ground. Being low protects them from wind. Many have waxy or hairy leaves. This helps keep water from releasing into the air so the plants don't dry out.

Some smartphone apps can identify flowers from a photo.

Wildflower Resources

Field guides help with flower identification.

People can use these books to look up flowers

by color and other features. Apps can also help.

Some apps are specialized for certain areas

or states. There are online wildflower databases. People can use apps to find and identify flowers near them. They can also add the flowers they see to the database.

Flowers are beautiful. There are many types. They grow in nearby parks and around the world. It is fun to find and identify flowers!

Explore Online

Explore the website below. What new information did you learn about wildflowers that wasn't in Chapter Three?

Native Plants of North America

abdocorelibrary.com/spotting-flowers

Field Notes

Magnifying glass

Camera

Sketchbook and pencil

Measuring tape

Wildflower Log

Name of flower:
Black-eyed Susan

Location:
Along park trail in a sunny spot

Time of year:
September

Height of plant:
Two feet
(0.6 m)

Stem texture:
Hairy

Leaf arrangement on stem:
Alternating along stem

Sketch:

Flower details:
Yellow flower, brown center. Two inches (5 cm) wide, ten petals in a disk

Leaf details:
Long, narrow leaves with smooth edges and covered in hairs

A blank Wildflower Log is available at **abdocorelibrary.com**.

Glossary

adaptations
qualities of a plant or animal that help it survive in its natural habitat

alpine
having to do with high mountains

camouflaged
hidden in one's surroundings

climate
the average weather in an area over a long period of time

elevation
the height above sea level

habitat
the natural environment where a plant or animal lives

pollinators
animals that help plants produce seeds by moving pollen from one flower to another

texture
the way a surface looks or feels

Online Resources

To learn more about spotting flowers, visit our free resource websites below.

Visit **abdocorelibrary.com** or scan this QR code for free Common Core resources for teachers and students, including vetted activities, multimedia, and booklinks, for deeper subject comprehension.

Visit **abdobooklinks.com** or scan this QR code for free additional online weblinks for further learning. These links are routinely monitored and updated to provide the most current information available.

Learn More

Bell, Samantha S. *Pollinator Gardens*. Abdo, 2026.

Cornell, Kari A. *Plant Projects*. Abdo, 2026.

Hoare, Ben. *The Secret World of Plants*. DK, 2022.

Index

About the Author

Laura Perdew is an author coach, presenter, and former teacher and the author of more than 60 fiction and nonfiction books for kids. She is also a big fan of wildflowers! One of her favorite things to do in the summer is to hike to a high alpine lake surrounded by wildflowers. She lives in Boulder, Colorado.